Y0-BCU-994

LITTLE

MONGRELS

With thanks to Anna Pignataro for the use of her handwriting

Konecky & Konecky
72 Ayers Point Rd.
Old Saybrook, CT 06475

This edition published by special arrangement with Lothian Books.

ISBN: 1-56852-584-2

Printed and bound in Hong Kong

LITTLE

DAVID DARCY

MONGRELS

KONECKY&KONECKY

Acknowledgements

This book has been a welcome challenge. It proved to be much harder to compile than I first expected and would not have been possible without the help of some puppy-loving individuals.

First and foremost, I would like to thank RSPCA Australia and staff members Jane Speechley, Mandy Richards, Karen Schliper, Bethany Livingston, Janelle Kalkan and Debbie Spencer. My thanks to you, not only for helping me with this book, but also for your dedication to saving animals. Words are not enough to describe the wonderful work you all do.

Many thanks to Sandra Stapley and her adorable little cattle dogs, who started this whole process; Kathy at Aaron Lodge, Blacktown City Animal Facility (remembering all dogs young and old); Frank from Salash; Rebecca and Nathan McCormack, the guys from Badgery's Creek and the happy horde of ridgebacks; and all the other people who let me into their homes to photograph their beautiful little puppies.

To all the farmers who allowed me onto their properties to photograph the working pups, I say thank you so much, with special thanks to Colin Seis, for his hospitality at Winona Stud in Gulgong. Special thanks also to Steve and Kim from Ilford, for the warm welcome and pleasant stay.

To Brett Wall: over the last few years we have photographed and filmed dogs in some amazing places — thanks for being there with me, mate. Finally, my thanks to all my friends and my family for their support and encouragement over the last six years: it has meant a lot.

Puppies from a big backyard

Little mongrels are a mixed bunch of wet-nosed puppies. They come from all walks of the dog world; they may be small or fat, shaggy-coated or 'blue'. Some of the breeds, such as border collies and cattle dogs, we recognise straight away; others are less distinguishable 'bitzers' (a bit of this and a bit of that), because their mum might be a Heinz-57 variety while their dad looks more like a goat than a dog. No matter how they appear, they all share the same wonderful puppy qualities: curiosity, adventurousness and loyalty. They are your best friend while you're around, smothering you with a sloppy tongue and puppy breath, but as soon as you're gone they're off down the backyard to explore and sniff out trouble.

Little mongrels have names like Rusty, Milly, Bonnie, Charlie, Jenny and Jess. Most of them look cute and adorable, like baby seals with their bulging brown eyes. But Boof the blue heeler pup has a big head like a baby wombat, and a fur coat like a dirty doormat. He doesn't care how he looks or whether his breath stinks as he struts around the yard, because he is the new king of his very own suburban jungle. Sally the little staffie is perfectly proportioned all over, except she has a set of ears from here to Christmas — two gigantic flaps on top of her brindle head.

These mini-mutts are born tough, ready for the rough and tumble of the Australian backyard. Take away all the soft toys and Barbie dolls, unless you want them chewed up; throw the little monsters a bone. There are no prissy pooches around here; ribbons are for chocolate boxes, not these little mongrels. These courageous pups are ready to slide down slippery dips and go billycart racing with their new best friend. They will wrestle with the hose in summer and chase a rake around the garden in autumn, bury a bone in the muddy garden in winter and chase the birds to no avail in spring.

Although time may have faded the stubborn stains your own puppy made on the carpet years ago, nothing can replace the memories of your four-legged

friend chewing up your shoes or tearing open the beanbag. Or the memories of that furry face and four oversized feet limp and sleepy on the couch; the whimpering sound at the door from your wet and muddy pup during a storm; the rush of little legs scurrying to keep up with you as you walk side-by-side; the two glassy eyes that looked up to you back then, and still look up to you today.

Growing up on the farm

Jessie is a three-year-old kelpie. She's a working dog and she's carrying her second litter of pups. At night she is locked in the machinery shed, where she has picked out a spot by the tractor to give birth to her new litter of pups. It's pitch dark in the shed, except for a beam of moonlight that falls through the window. This night nine little rat-sized pups are born on the dusty floor. Jessie instinctively sets about cleaning each of her young. In those first few hours the nine small kelpies get their first taste of dust, straw and diesel fumes as their life on the land begins.

The farmer supplies Jessie and her new pups with a comfortable cardboard box in the corner of the shed. Jessie cares for the pups, feeding and cleaning them regularly. Just to be safe, Jessie also keeps the other farm dogs away. The puppies grow fast on their mother's milk, and they kick, wriggle and roll around in their box all day long.

At five weeks of age the puppies begin to wander from their box and find their way into trouble. The farmer moves all the pups into an old disused chicken shed, and here behind the chicken wire they are safe from harm. A 44-gallon drum that has been cut in half lengthwise becomes their round-roofed kennel, and an old hubcap becomes their dinner plate. Two chewed-up buckets are used for their drinking water; they look as though they've gone under the tractor a couple of times, but their worn appearance is simply due to the sharp little teeth of last year's litter. A couple of lengths of rope lying in the dirt will make excellent toys for the young pups when they're a little older.

By eight weeks of age the puppies have become more independent. Some pups fight among themselves to become the top pup; others sniff around the old wooden boxes where the chooks used to lay their eggs, and they find plenty of cobwebs; a couple of pups try to sleep on a dusty piece of foam rubber. Each day at dusk the puppies are let out into the yard for an hour, where they run and play frantically. Jessie and the two other adult dogs that have been out in the paddock working all day lie watchfully on the back of the truck, out of reach of the little mongrels. The older workers observe the puppies chasing each other around the shed and under the truck.

When the farmer brings the dinner buckets, the atmosphere changes instantly. The older dogs sit upright and stare at the approaching feast, as the smell of fresh meat and dog biscuits fills the air; the nine young adventurers come running from every corner of the yard, barking and yapping up a storm as they dance at the farmer's feet. The farmer walks on and throws the buckets up onto the back of the truck. He rewards his three older working dogs, first with a quick but endearing pat on the head before a chicken carcass is given to each of them. The dogs take their meals to separate corners of the utility tray, then lie down to eat.

By this time, the nine little mongrels at the farmer's feet are in a frenzy, their barks turning to howls as though they haven't eaten all day; but that morning, just like every morning, they had a milky porridge for breakfast. The farmer picks up the puppies' dinner bucket and ushers them back into the old chicken shed, where there is a flurry of heads and feet in the dinner bowl, and tails in the air. Their dinner is all over in a few seconds and the farmer shuts the gate, locking up the pups for the night.

These pups are now ready for new homes, and some will be sold to other farmers in the area. A few will begin to learn how to work the sheep; later, when they're fully trained, they'll be sold to other farmers as working dogs. A couple of lucky pups will remain to see out their working lives on the farm where they were born.

Hound Street

It's daybreak and light begins to filter through the laundry window, revealing the room's contents: a washing machine and dryer, a basin filled with dirty clothes and, on the floor in the corner, a sleeping puppy. She is curled up tightly into a ball of fluff, her small face and snout tucked in under her two front legs. She lies on top of a pastel-pink blanket; newspaper covers the floor around her bedding. The pup looks more like a stuffed toy than a dog as she lies motionless on her cosy, warm bed.

The first sounds of distant traffic drone through the double-brick walls as the puppy begins to stir. It's 6.00 a.m. and the house is still and quiet, but it's the calm before the storm. Saturday is always a busy day in the Johnson household and this day is even more special, because last night Dad brought home a new addition to the family: a ten-week-old pup. The three Johnson kids, Rhiannon who is twelve, Jade who is nine and Matthew who is seven, could hardly contain themselves last night as they cuddled and played with the new pup. It was after midnight before all the children were marched off to their rooms and the puppy was put to bed in the laundry.

As the first set of footsteps come slapping down the stairs, the puppy wakes and sits upright. The little dog stares at the door, her head tilted to one side. She tries to prick up her ears, but they are not yet strong enough and they quickly flop down again. The door bursts open and Rhiannon rushes in. The puppy jumps up to greet the girl, its little tail beating quickly. The girl lifts her puppy into the air, cuddling it. The puppy responds with a lick to her face and a wiggle. Rhiannon whispers to the puppy, 'You're not a dream!'

It doesn't take long before the whole family is awake and they gather together in the lounge room. The puppy takes centre stage on the floor as they all sit around and laugh. They agree that her name will be 'Molly'.

This Saturday is the first of many Saturdays the family will spend with Molly. Over the years Molly will become a much-loved member of the Johnson household and will become part of their family history. Molly will be there when Rhiannon has her sixteenth birthday party in the backyard. During the speech Molly will jump up on the table and lick the birthday cake, much to the amusement of the whole party, except Mum. When Jade gets glandular fever in Year Nine, Molly will sit by her side while the doctors come and go for several months. After Jade recovers, Molly will sleep protectively at the foot of Jade's bed every night for the next two years, until Jade moves into the spare room upstairs. When Matthew buys his first car at the age of nineteen, Molly will be the first to go for a drive with him. On that day, Matthew will drive down to the local river where he will take Molly for a short walk; and Molly will run up to a lovely young stranger who Matthew will marry three years later.

Molly is a new chapter in the lives of this family. She will delight and entertain three small children as they grow, giving them love and affection as only a dog knows how. She will be in many of the pictures of the kids playing together in the family photo album. She will feature in the family's home videos, as the children become teenagers and go to high school. In their hearts, Molly will continue to be part of the family, even after old age takes her from them.

▲ *Big night.*

◀ *My dad's in the construction industry.*

Charlie, the cattle dog

While Mum's asleep I'm in charge.

The Boss

▲ *Where did I leave my playlunch?*

▶ *He shoots. He scores!*

Mini mates

For five-week-old Chip the kelpie, size is a problem. His legs are like chicken wings, his nose is the size of a Smartie and his toughest bark is just a timid yap. Life is a little intimidating because everything around him is so big. People look like giants as they stomp around with big hands that grab him, big mouths that kiss him and monstrous feet that nearly tread on his tail. All this makes a five-week-old puppy very shy. Finding friends the same size is difficult as well. The little birds in the garden don't want to play, and the sound of another dog's bark makes him nervous. Even the darned cat is bigger than him.

The first few weeks of life are an anxious time for such a small pup. It's best for him to be a little cautious and wait until he's able to run about without tripping over his own feet before facing the unknown. Until then, having a name like Bruiser, Buster or Tex just might make him feel braver.

▲ *What does that fur ball do up here all day?*

▶ *Please don't look in the garden.*

Lance, the mongrel

▲ *Did you hear the one about …?*

◀ *Waiting for my birthday.*

▲ *Pooch pillow.*

▲ *There must be a leak in the roof.*

▶ *Wrongly accused.*

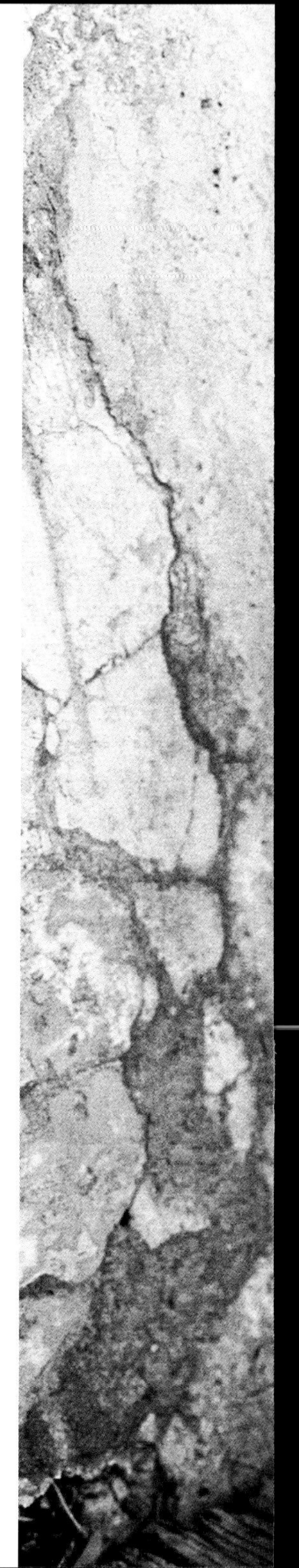

Ute life

Personally, I like growing up in the ute. It may not look very flash to you cushion-bound city pups, but it's home to me. Growing up in the ute has its advantages too. I can have a snooze any time I like and my best friend can't take off without me. I can chew up sticks and slobber all over the place and I don't get in any trouble. If I have an 'accident' in the back, my mate just hoses off the tray and the ute is as good as new. If it's hot outside, my mate parks our ute in the shade, so the tray is nice and cool.

I can scratch at the floor of the ute and bite on all the empty plastic bottles back there. I can yap at the cat that hangs around the house and he won't bother me up here in the ute.

When my mate takes me to work, I wait in the back and at lunch his friends give me their leftovers. On the way home I stick my head over the side and let my tongue flap in the breeze. If I'm lucky the wind will blow bugs into my mouth. On Fridays we park at the pub for a short while, which is great because I can sit up and chat to my doggy mates in the other utes.

The best part about life in the ute is knowing that it's my home. I go where the ute goes and my friend always knows where to find me, so we're never far apart.

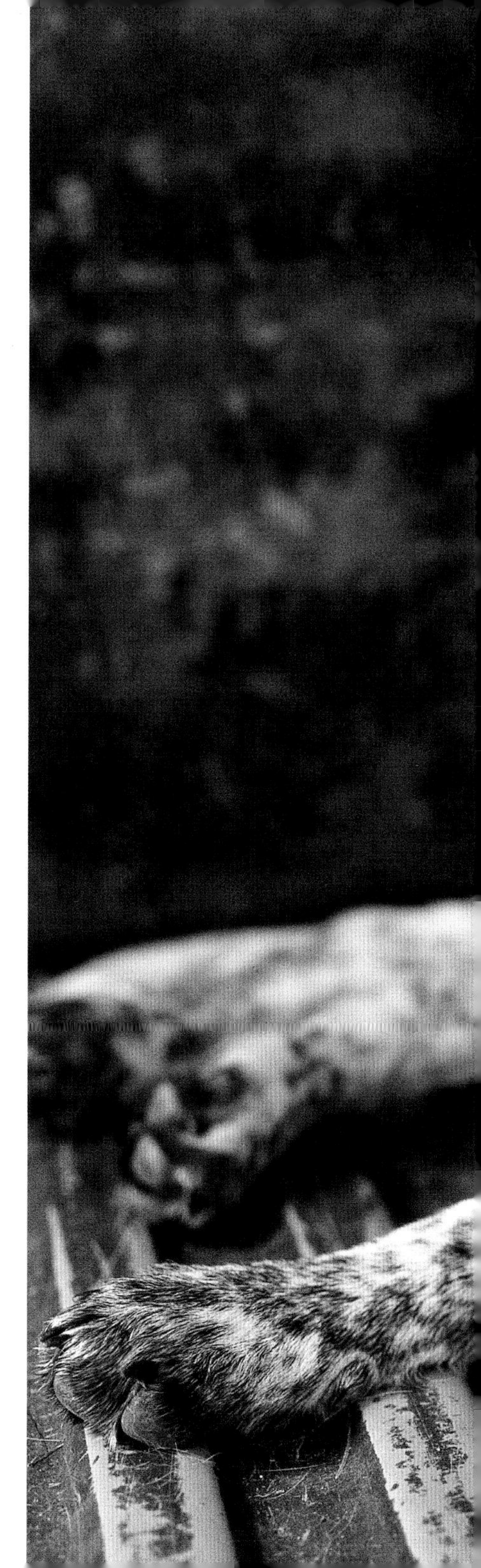

Using all five senses

Looking for trouble

If it crawls like a spider, slides like a snake or jumps like a frog it must be interesting. Regardless of the consequences, a curious pup like Bob the Jack Russell is eager to find out all about the world around him. Some little dogs just can't help themselves. They just have to stick their tiny wet noses where they don't belong. Bob's interests don't just stop at critters. He's also eager to pry into your cheese and pickle sandwich — not to eat it, but to check what kind of cheese it is. But Bob has his reasons for sticking his snout into other people's business. Puppies are curious creatures by nature.

Otherwise, how would they know whether or not the cushions on the sofa are dangerous? The only way to find out about cushions is to chew them up until the stuffing comes out. The lesson is: if it doesn't bite back, it's safe. As the saying goes, 'Curiosity killed the cat.' Know what I mean, Bob?

Tastes like chicken ...

Guess which team won?

Better tidy yourself up, looks like we've got company.

Cartoons after school.

Tastes better than dirt.

Little
Mongrels

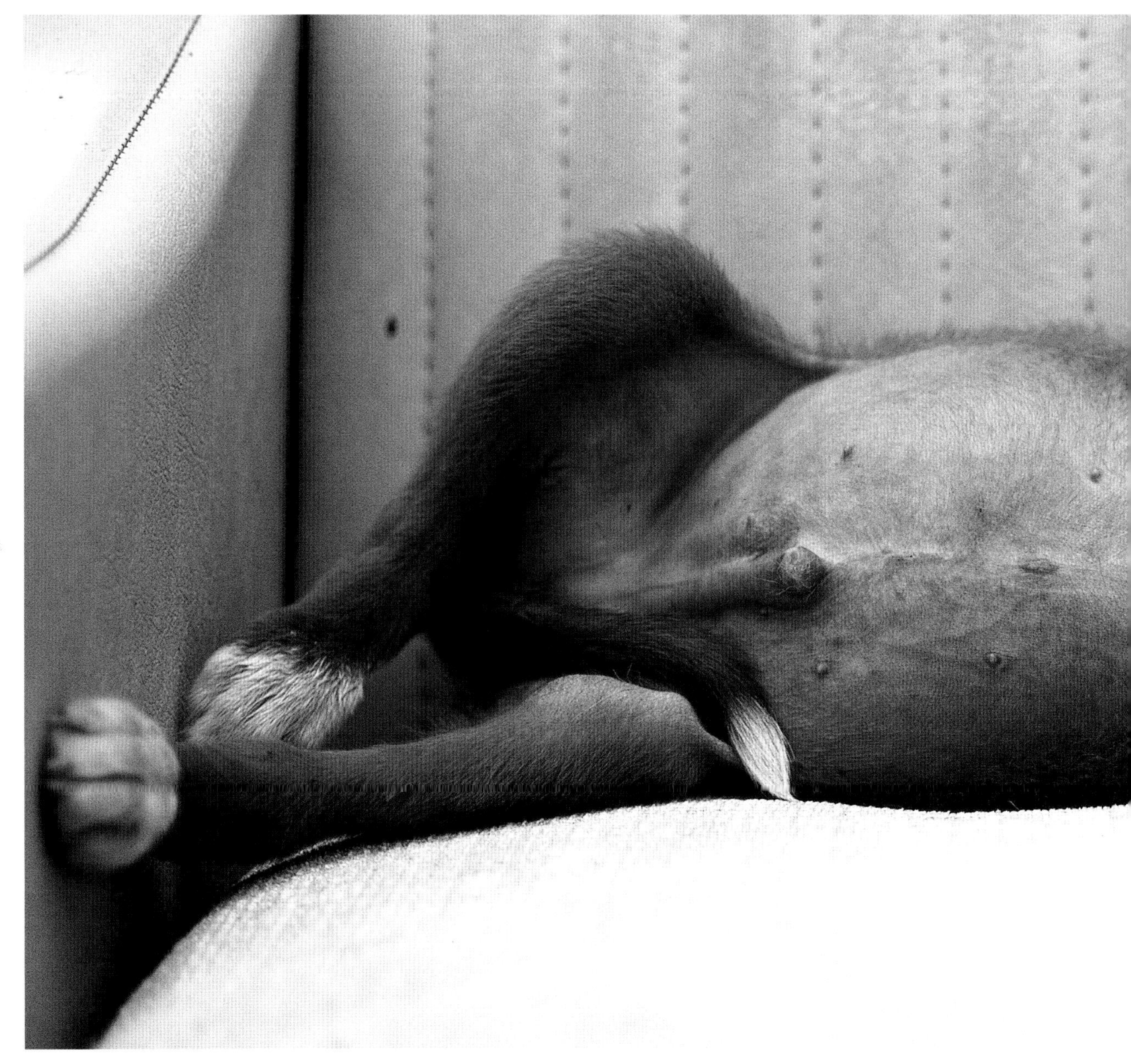

I think my eyes were bigger than my belly.

Benny and Joon, star-crossed Labradors

▲ *The three o'clock sugar slump.*

◀ *One for the family photo album.*

of his puppy life. He can spend his day chewing up cardboard, eating strange objects and annoying the cat. Time is short and he needs to make the most of his destructive youth, so he begins by getting into the garbage.

Garbage bins are full of all sorts of wonderful treats for a naughty puppy. They contain plastic bags full of stinky left-overs, smelly scraps of meat, rotten fruit, slimy eggshells and mouldy bread. A pup will tip the bin over and when he has finished spreading rubbish around the house, he'll find a good spot in the corner of the lounge room to leave his mark. Once he's feeling relieved, he'll go out into the garden and dig a hole somewhere. When his paws are still dirty, he'll quickly run back inside the house across the clean carpet, which he finds most satisfying. In the afternoon he'll pull the washing off the line, chew up a shoe and finally hide under the house. His day is complete.

Begins in jest

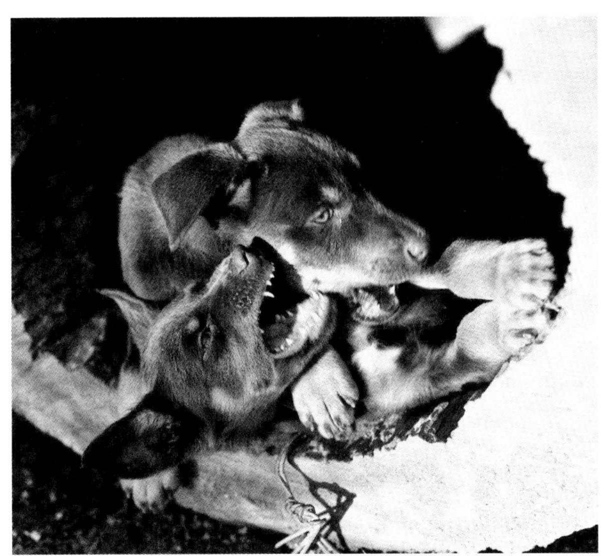

… ends in tears.

Felix and Oscar, an odd pair of hounds

▲ *Winners are grinners.*

◀ *My tongue is longer than yours!*

Are you just going to stand there, or are you going to give me a hand?

Bathtime! No one will find me here.

Hide and seek in the old cattle yard

Chewed shoes

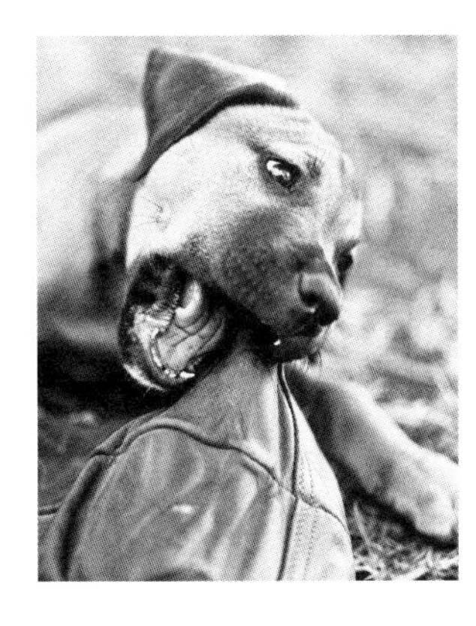

Shoes and socks are the enemy; they must be destroyed. Shoes turn up in plenty of different places, so beware. The best way to engage in combat with a shoe is to go for its soft spot. This is called the sock. Take the sock from the shoe and hold it down with both paws. Using your sharpest teeth, thrash at the sock until it starts to make a tearing sound. This will result in what humans call a 'hole'. Once the sock has a hole in it, it is done for. Repeat this process for the second sock. Once you're sure the coast is clear, you can then move on to the shoe. There are many kinds of shoes and the more expensive ones are the best to destroy. First, grab the shoe by the tongue. This is the weakest part of the shoe and the easiest part to damage. Chew, tear and rip at the tongue until it resembles something the cat dragged in. Then get your head inside the opening of the shoe, which can be tricky. Once inside, you will find a soft, sponge-like sole. This sole must be pulled out and chewed into little pieces. Then the shoe will be useless. Remember, you are only a puppy once and while you're young you can get away with destroying as many shoes as you like. Once you're past the puppy stage it's best to take the shoe and bury it in the backyard. Good luck!

Bedroom renovation

Peace and quiet

When little puppies fall asleep in the sunshine, what do they dream about? Do they dream about digging giant holes in the soft, warm sand, rolling around in the daisies on a grassy hillside or chasing blind three-legged cats? Do they dream about getting everything they want? Do they want more toys or do they need more blankets in their beds? And if they do dream, do they remember their dreams when they wake up?

I imagine that eight-week-old Jenny the labrador pup only dreams about food: mountains of glistening meat and rivers of beef gravy. She must also dream about being let loose in the butcher's shop, sprawling out over the rib-cutlets. Or perhaps she imagines herself running through a desert to reach a white oasis, a lake of full-cream milk. Labrador puppies might even dream about starring in movies such as *Willy Wonka & the Chocolate Factory*, only with bones and biscuits instead of chocolate.

Great little Danes

Roll over, you're snoring again.

Keep your nose to the ground and your ear to the wall.

Sleeping safely

▲ *Harry sleeps while the others gossip.*

◀ *No vacancies.*

It's been a big morning.

I always get the bottom bunk.

Bed bug

Another balmy night on the porch in my hessian bed. The air is so still. It's so quiet out here. I can still smell on my whiskers the mince and milk I had for dinner. The porch light shines bright like the moon, way up above my bed. I hear a strange buzzing in the distance. It sounds like a lawnmower, but it's pitch dark outside. No one could be mowing at this hour. I prick my ears and listen carefully. The buzz gets louder and louder. I sit up and stare into the dark and listen. It's coming straight towards me. Then I make out what it is. It's a big black beetle. It swoops in like a busted old aeroplane and lands near the light. It is the biggest beetle I have ever seen and as I stare at it in disbelief it falls down behind the old cane chair. Ever so cautiously I crawl under the chair to take a closer look. At first I can't find it, but then it appears and starts to crawl towards me. I back away from it, slowly at first, but then a little too quickly and bump my head on the chair. The monster beetle keeps crawling towards me. I bounce back a few steps and bark at it. But the beetle keeps coming. I run back towards my bed. The beetle keeps coming. I jump behind the pot plant and peer around the side and the beetle keeps coming. I tell myself, 'This is it, I must prepare myself for battle.'

At just the right moment I pounce on it. 'Ah ha!' I wait a second or two and then slowly open my paws. 'Oh, no, it's gone.' I look around frantically, but the beetle is nowhere to be seen. Then my worst nightmare is realised: I feel it crawling on my back. 'Ahhhhhhh.' I jump and yelp; I roll and bark. I hear a buzzing sound and stop. The seconds tick by. 'Tick, tick, tick.' It's gone. Thank goodness. As I wander back to my bed I look under the chair just to make sure. I jump back into bed and lie down, keeping one eye open for the rest of the night.

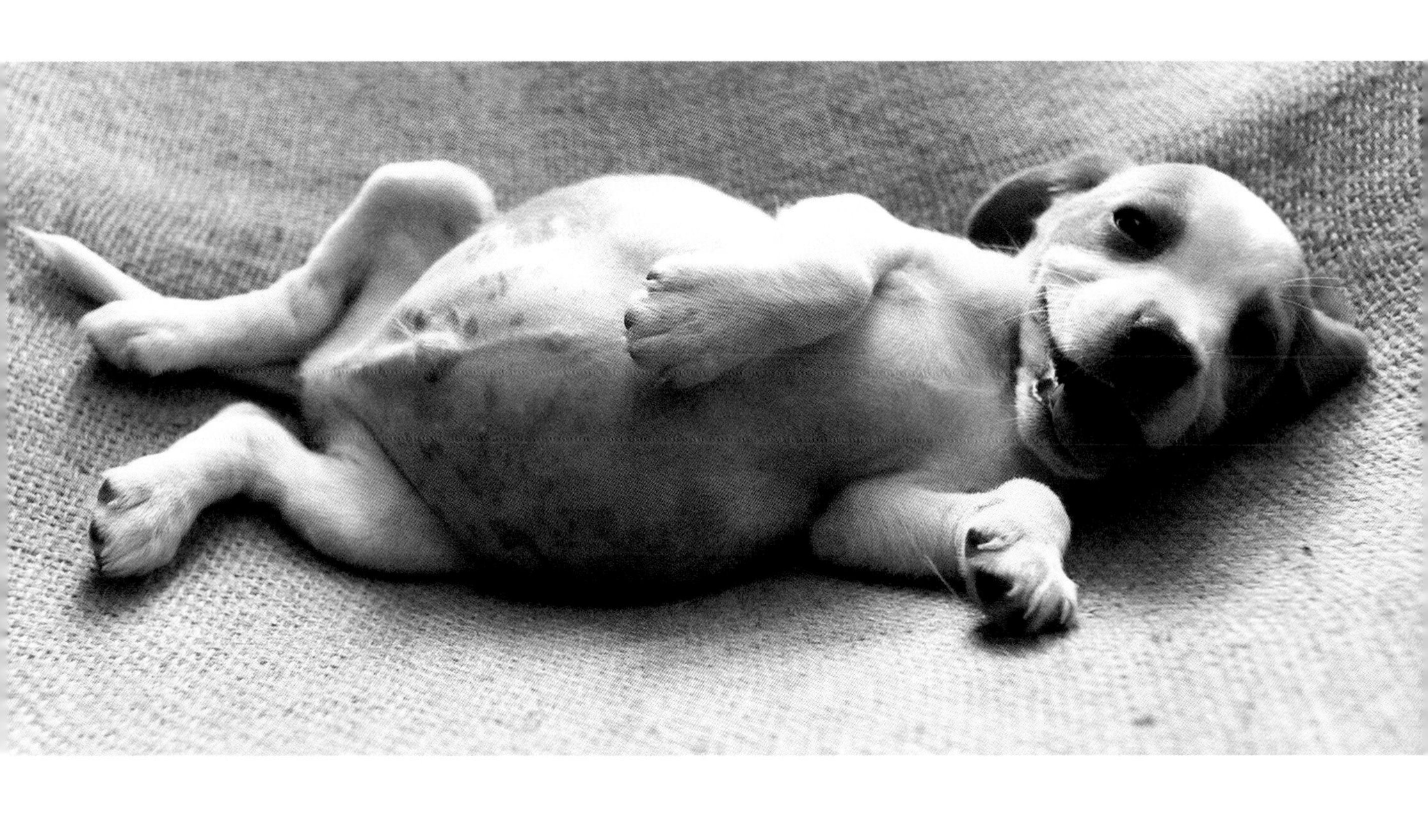

Australian-made workers

Courage plays a big role in the life of Nipper the kelpie. Born to be brave, he is rough, ready, fearless and energetic.

The life of a working dog in the country starts early, and at daybreak a little eight-week-old pup waits patiently behind the chicken wire. The farmer starts his truck — the signal that the day's work has begun. The older dogs run and jump up onto the back of the ute. The older dogs have been working this land for many years. The little guy behind the wire gets ready to do the same thing, but a helping hand sees that he doesn't get any big ideas: he'll ride in the front with the farmer until he's big enough to handle himself on the back of the truck. Little working dogs have a lot to live up to, whether they're kelpies, cattle dogs, border collies or mongrels. Over the years, this little kelpie will acquire the skills and the strength that he was bred for — those required for mustering sheep and rounding up stubborn cattle. Soon enough he will be working the stock around the paddock with his older mates.

Around the woolshed

Keep an eye on those sheep, mate!

Thank heavens I don't have to shear 'em.

With all of us this'll be easy.

It's doggone hard work!

Little
Mongrels

The natural

▲ *The leader of the gang.*

◀ *Ready for the ambush.*

Wagging in the sheep yard

Kennel Kindness

What could be more heart-warming than to see puppies cuddled up together? Like Sam and Jerome, the two small chocolate-coloured mongrels meeting in their kennel on the verandah. They have been playing around in the grass all morning, fighting and wrestling together. But now they're tired and any quarrels are forgiven. One dog checks the other to make sure all is well. They just need the reassurance of each other's company while they rest.

Puppies bring out a sense of tenderness in us. Whether it's their loyal stare as they sit longingly at a window, waiting for our return, or a sympathetic paw reaching out carefully to touch our hand, they make us feel important. Their slightest antics touch us. And it's all those warm feelings that help us to forgive their misbehaviour as they sit looking up at us all bent-eared and wide-eyed. Puppies need our tender love and care, which they return tenfold.

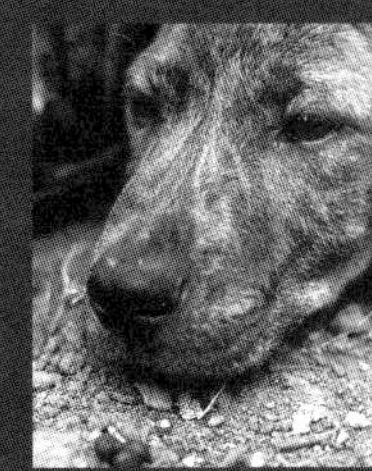

▲ *It just needs a coat of paint.*

▶ *When I grow up, I'll guard it with my life.*

Did you wash behind your ears?

Spot and Digger, best friends

Sheep counters.

Best friends

Buddy the Jack Russell doesn't complain about the way he looks. He doesn't care whether or not he's having a bad hair day.

Puppies don't mind what people think about their looks, and they don't care how you look either. At seven weeks of age Buddy is not much bigger than a hamburger, and weighs less than a can of soft drink. But he knows how to be loyal. A little pup can be the best mate of a builder, or a nurse who works all night long. He is just as happy to be friends with a homeless person as he is to be friends with someone who owns a big house. He plays games with you whether you're seven years old or seventy. And will always love you no matter how you look. That is what makes Buddy so special. Even though he is just a little pup, he will always accept you no matter who you are, what you do or where you come from.

Buddy, the Jack Russell

Down by the dam

He looks just like his grandad

My best mate

I remember the day we first met. It was late afternoon on a Saturday. While a dozen other little puppies played and yapped, you just sat and stared at me. I wanted to take all of the pups home that day, but I chose you and I'm so glad that I did. I picked you up and you licked my face. I laughed and your tail wagged. I remember thinking how innocent and adorable you were and that I just wanted to look after you.

As the weeks passed you grew strong and confident. We played fetch in the park and you chased stick after stick. At the beach you ran up and down the shoreline like a fool. When I went swimming you would follow me out into the surf. Sometimes the waves crashed on your head, which scared you and you went back to the beach.

Sometimes while I was at work you got bored. You chewed a hole in my backpack and tore up the rug. You got into the garbage countless times. You even mangled a pair of my good boots. I got angry with you and yelled at you, telling you what a bad dog you were, but the naughty things you did mean nothing to me now. I should have known better, not you.

I left my regular job to pursue the work I loved and we were able to spend more time together. We began to travel all over the country. You sat in the back of the ute; it was your ute and no one could touch it. We camped in the bush and at night you fossicked for scraps around the fire. Sometimes you got too close to the fire and singed your whiskers. During the day we wandered through farmyards and country towns.

Time passed and several more puppies joined you at home in the yard. You spent all day chasing each other around the kennels or wrestling in the garden. The puppies grew up fast and it wasn't long before the whole mob of us began to travel as a team and follow my dreams again. You never complained or appeared to be unhappy; you just wagged your tail with excitement. It helped reaffirm what a special creature you are.

I went overseas for a while. I had tears in my eyes and a lump in my throat when I had to say goodbye to you. After I left, you waited at the door for me every day, or so I was told. While I was overseas people would ask me if I was homesick and I told them that I missed you. I came back six months later and you

were still waiting for me at the back door. You treated me as though I'd never left: you bore me no grudge and were not angry with me or jealous. We were best mates again.

As the years passed, people came and went. But I could always count on you. You are the reason I am who I am. When you were young, you helped me to realise what love brings to a life. You never judge me when I'm wrong. You never ignore me after I have ignored you. You are so loyal in a world so cruel, and I know you would give your life to save mine. You will never know how much you have changed my life or how grateful I am that you are my best mate.

Dave